About the Author and the Book

Polly Lloyd is a well-known voice on Westcountry radio.
She lives in Bristol with her husband, two children, two cats and two goldfish. A Scorpio subject, she was born in Liverpool and came to Bristol at the age of fourteen, when her family moved to the city. Polly Lloyd joined BBC Radio Bristol as a secretary in 1981. 'Then, one day, I was asked to read a listener's letter on air, and instinctively knew: "This is what I want to do!"' She is currently presenting the Teatime Show, each weekday afternoon. Her interests include the theatre, dance and opera, and history in any shape or form. Until recently she was a member of an amateur dance group, which raised money for charity. In 1987 she visited Egypt and produced and presented a BBC Radio Bristol cassette on Ancient Egypt and Egypt today. This is Polly's first book, and she is at present researching a second book about strange stories – to be published by Bossiney in 1989.

Dorset is a mine of myth and folklore – so much so that some of the legends have become part of the Dorset landscape. Here, Polly Lloyd explores legendary Dorset, visiting places as diverse as the Sacred Circle at Knowlton and Chesil Beach. She tells of stones that turn at cockcrow and ghostly dogs who haunt country lanes. She recalls, too, real people who have become legends – contrasting characters like Lillie Langtry, mistress to Edward VII, and infamous Judge Jeffreys. Polly Lloyd also turns detective and examines the possible link between Dorset and Jack the Ripper. Specially commissioned photographs by Rob Scott and drawings by Felicity Young all combine to make this a memorable journey.

Legends of
DORSET

POLLY LLOYD

BOSSINEY BOOKS

First published in 1988 by
Bossiney Books
St Teath, Bodmin, Cornwall.

Typeset and Printed by
Clowes Book Printers
St Columb, Cornwall.

ISBN 0 948158 44 1

Front cover: River Frome at County Bridge
near Wool
Back cover: The coastline near
Lulworth Cove

PLATE ACKNOWLEDGMENTS
Cover photography by Roy J. Westlake
Rob Scott: pages 7, 11, 23, 30, 32, 37, 38, 41,
42, 43, 44, 49, 50, 52, 60, 64, 67, 68, 71, 76,
84, 85, 91, 93, 95
Felicity Young: pages 13, 14, 19, 25, 55, 59,
78, 82, 87, 90
Roy J. Westlake: pages 6, 8, 21, 22, 54, 56
Paul Honeywill: pages 73, 75
BBC Radio Bristol: page 4
Ray Bishop: page 28
Peter Friend: page 34

Legends of Dorset

The folklore of Dorset has become part of the landscape. Old tales and the art of story-telling have combined to fascinate both local people and visitors – so much so that you begin to wonder whether there can be such a thing as total myth.

This then is a journey through legendary Dorset.

And how richly the traveller is rewarded. Rolling downs, lush green vales, golden beaches, Dorset has them all. Seaside resorts, comfortable towns and picturesque villages, there is hardly an ugly corner to be found. Timeless order and security in the form of mellow stone, brick and thatch, neat streets and cottage gardens. In the search for the perfect English county, Dorset must rate pretty high. Even the place names have a magical ring to them – Blandford Forum, Okeford Fitzpaine, Litton Cheney.

But it would be a mistake to regard Dorset simply as a picture-book place where time has stood still. Self-contained is not the same as closed; timeless means classic rather than old-fashioned. Far from standing still, layer upon layer of history has shaped Dorset and continues to do so. And the stories of the people and the places who played their part have been told down all the years.

Stories of courage and treachery, of fairies and witches. Tales of kings and highwaymen and holy saints. And strange accounts of stones that turn at cockcrow, dogs that haunt country lanes and stolen church bells that lie deep in mill ponds.

Every part of Dorset seems to have its own story. Some are based on the geography of the land, like the magnificent sweep of the pebble

LEFT **The Author Polly Lloyd.**

5

beach at Chesil. Others centre on the landmarks left by the earliest inhabitants, such as the famous chalk hill figure, the Cerne Abbas Giant. Then there are tales of characters who are remembered because they were cruel or brave or beautiful, people like Lillie Langtry, mistress of Edward VII who lived in Bournemouth. Such characters may belong to reality, but, by their lives, they have become *legendary* personalities, and therefore belong to the Folklore of Dorset.

It is a county that has inspired many authors. Jane Austen was particularly fond of Lyme Regis, making the Cobb as famous for being

RIGHT 'The folklore of Dorset has become part of the landscape.'

BELOW Gold Hill, Shaftesbury: 'In the search for the perfect English county Dorset must rate pretty high.'

the place where Louisa Musgrove fell in *Persuasion* as it is for being the landing point for the Duke of Monmouth at the start of his ill-fated rebellion. John Fowles also chose Lyme Regis as the setting for his modern classic *The French Lieutenant's Woman*. And, of course, Thomas Hardy, arguably Dorset's most famous son, wrote wonderfully evocative accounts of life here.

But apart from these great works of fiction, Dorset is a treasure house of stories, happy and sad, funny and macabre. Time has occasionally blurred the edges between fact and fantasy, and some of the tales are hard to prove – but just as hard to disprove. Some are as old as time while one or two happened within living memory. But all of them add to the richness of history, these legends of Dorset.

BELOW 'Even the place names have a magical ring
... Litton Cheney.'

RIGHT '... a county that has inspired many
authors. Jane Austen was particularly fond of
Lyme Regis.'

Fairies, Witches and Strange Creatures

In days gone by, when life was less exacting, there was time to ponder on the vagaries of the world about us, time indeed to notice the curious happenings that serve to remind us that 'there are more things in heaven and earth . . . than are dreamt of in your philosophy.'

Stories must be told, and tales recounted, and if science and logic fail to provide a satisfactory explanation, the answer must lie elsewhere. Even today those who like to keep an open mind on these matters can see that perhaps after all we share this planet with other less restricted beings.

It's dangerous stuff, of course, because people who like scientific and logical explanations are easily frightened by such free spirits and down the ages they have tried to stamp out any line of thinking which differed from their own and thereby threatened their authority. Consequently people who communicated with fairies, or worse still, indulged in witchcraft, white or black, were severely dealt with. Friends and neighbours with less of an axe to grind were scared of the witches but more sympathetic about the fairies and other strange creatures which inhabited the countryside.

In the 1560s a man called John Walsh of Netherbury, near Beaminster, was sent to trial for witchcraft. It was said that he consorted with fairies, who he believed lived in prehistoric burial mounds, and that he had spoken with the Devil himself. We don't know what happened to John Walsh, although he was almost certainly horribly tortured during his interrogation, but we do have a contemporary record of what he said.

RIGHT **Polly Lloyd at Ashmore.**

10

He being demanded how he knoweth when anye man is bewitched: He sayth that he knew it partlye by the Feries, white green and black. Which when he is disposed to vse, hee speaketh with them vpon hyls, where as there is great heapes of earth, as namely in Dorsetshire. And betwene the houres of xii and one at noone, or at midnight he vseth them. Whereof he sayth the blacke Feries be the woorst.

Barrows or burial mounds were popularly believed to be the homes of fairies. The barrow at Washers Pit near Fontmell Magna was well known for the curious sounds around it until after 4,000 years the barrow was removed in 1840 to make way for a road. The ancient bones found in it were reburied in Ashmore churchyard. The fairies, or Gabbygammies as they were known, moved as well, also to

Ashmore to the village pond, an idyllic setting as anyone who knows it will agree.

More fairies are to be found, if legend is to be believed, at Stourpaine Church in Blandford Forum. Evidently these fairies like to ring the church bells and tiptoe up to the belfry while the dew is still fresh on the grass. If they see a mortal footprint, they turn back and lay a curse of ill-fortune on the person who has spoiled their fun. But people say that if you visit the church just after the dew has gone, you can see tiny drops on the stone steps, a sure sign that the fairies have visited undisturbed.

Incidentally, Dorset fairies, it would seem, are far from silent, making a characteristic eerie noise which fills the air with a sort of chattering, hence the name Gabbygammies, or Gappergammies. But the words have other connections, for instance with birds, gapmouth being an old Dorset name for the nightjar, while further afield in other parts of the country, Gabbleratchets are hunting dogs which cause a sort of aerial noise.

In Dorset, too, dogs have their own special place in folklore. There are numerous tales of ghostly canines – invariably large and black with glowing eyes – and some areas have their 'own' dog – the Row Dog which wanders around Portland, and the Roy dog which haunts a cave near Portland Bill. Dogs were often regarded as a portent of death, walking beside some poor unsuspecting victim along a country road, or appearing unexpectedly in a cottage room shortly before one of the occupants shuffled off this mortal coil. One can't help wondering, of course, whether the sudden appearance of a large black dog might be enough to nudge those of a nervous disposition into an early grave, and that perhaps the reputation as an omen of doom is circumstantial.

There are happier tales connected with these animals however. One concerns a farmer whose house near Lyme was regularly visited by a black dog. The two would sit quite amicably either side of the fire each evening. Other people warned the farmer to get rid of the dog, but he didn't really want to challenge it and this comfortable state of affairs went on for some time. One night, however, the farmer got

RIGHT **'Roy Dog which haunts a cave near Portland Bill.'**

12

drunk at the local inn, and spurred on by his drinking companions and full of Dutch courage, he went home and chased the dog around the house brandishing a poker at it. The dog ran upstairs to the attic and with a mighty leap sprang up through the ceiling. The farmer struck a hole in the ceiling with his poker – and out fell an ancient box full of gold and silver coins. The dog never returned to the farmhouse but haunts a nearby road, known ever since as Dog Lane.

There are tales of another strange creature that roamed the Dorset countryside – a fine, free, wild colt with green eyes known as Lazy Lawrence. Why 'lazy' it's hard to say, for Lawrence's task was to guard the orchards, chasing away anyone with a mind for pixying or scrumping the apples. Those with a clear conscience might see him galloping very fast in the moonlight, but if he fixed you with his green eyes, you were rooted to the spot.

Lazy Lawrence, let me goo
Don't hold me summer and winter too.

Lazy Lawrence took good care of those who looked after him. There was once a farmer's widow who sold apples from her two fine orchards at Wareham market. Each evening, she would leave out a 'dish of cream and a pail of spring water' for Lazy Lawrence. A wicked conjurer was envious of the widow and decided to use his powers to gain the apples for himself. He cast a spell on the trees, and then with great cunning, hid himself inside an apple hamper and rolled into the orchard, safe – or so he thought – from Lazy Lawrence's knowing gaze. The apples fell from the trees in a great magic circle, but some landed on the conjurer himself, causing him to jump out of the hamper and come face to face with Lazy Lawrence. The handsome colt chased him round the orchard until eventually he fixed him with a glare from his wild green eyes and the conjurer was rooted to the spot.

The next morning the widow came to the orchard with her helpers to pick the fruit. What a sight greeted them. All the apples lay in a great circle on the ground and in the middle stood the conjurer,

LEFT **Lazy Lawrence, a strange creature who roamed the Dorset countryside.**

15

stiff as a scarecrow and bitten and kicked. In the dew on the grass could be see a ring of hoofmarks. How they all laughed at the spell-bound conjurer until gradually the sun dried the dew and at last he was free to run away. They say he's running still from Lazy Lawrence.

★ ★ ★

Dorset, like any other county, has had its share of witches, and stories of witchcraft continued long after John Walsh was sent to trial in the sixteenth century. In 1884 the Petty Sessions at Sherborne were called upon to pass judgment on a woman who had attacked her neighbour, scratching the old woman with a needle and drawing blood, because she believed she had 'overlooked' her child, causing the infant to become ill. The court, it seems, were not impressed by this explanation, and fined the unhappy mother for assault.

This belief that one could be released from a spell or curse by literally blood-letting was common, and there are other records of people scratching the supposed witch with a needle and rubbing their own hand in the blood. People who had been bewitched suffered in various ways, some more dramatic than others. The victim might have a run of bad luck, or go into a state of gradual decline, or he might experience violent pains or even fits. Sometimes these attacks were accompanied by apparitions; sometimes evil charms were discovered hidden in the house or in their clothing.

Animals too could be 'overlooked' – a farmer once offended a bad-tempered old hag by demanding a higher price for some of the pigs she was buying from him on the grounds that they were bigger than the others and worth more money. The old woman flew into a rage and refused to buy any at all, cursing the farmer as she stormed off. Within a fortnight all the pigs, fine, strong creatures each of them, had mysteriously died. And this is not a tale from hundreds of years ago – this is a story from the beginning of this century. The old superstitions die hard.

Sceptics of course will say it's all a lot of stuff and nonsense, and mark it down to coincidence or ignorance or over-imagination. And it's not easy to draw the line between a 'wise woman' who knows how to use the herbs and plants to soothe and restore, and the lonely, unpopular old harridan who can conveniently be blamed for any number of misfortunes which may befall a community. And if the innocent can be wrongly accused, how easy it must be for someone

16

with malicious intent to frighten gullible neighbours. Minds already open to persuasion are soon led to regard simple trickery as magic.

And yet there are occasions when individuals who really ought to be able to resist the implications of witchcraft are nevertheless unable to offer any other explanation for strange events. Perhaps the most famous of these in Dorset is the story of the Reverend William Ettrick, vicar of Affpuddle and Turner's Puddle at the beginning of the nineteenth century. An intelligent and educated man, the entries in his diary from February 1804 until the following January record his growing belief in – and fear of – witchcraft.

Affpuddle and Turner's Puddle lie not far from Tolpuddle, close by the River Piddle or Trent. Puddle is presumably a corruption of the old word *pidele* meaning fast running stream. Affpuddle is a typically attractive Dorset village; Turner's Puddle a tiny hamlet, difficult to find, with two fords keeping the outside world at bay. The small church at Turner's Puddle is disused now; the only sound comes from the rooks calling to each other in the treetops high above the ivy-clad churchyard.

The Reverend Ettrick's problems began with the arrival of a woman called Susan Woodrow who was employed to work in the vicarage garden. She was chosen because she was known to have powers with plants and vegetables and it was hoped the garden would flourish under her care. Mr Ettrick's diary tells us Susan arrived on 23 February – four days later his young, strong horse fell ill. At first, the vicar made no connection. Indeed, shortly afterwards, Susan herself became ill and was away from the vicarage for some weeks. The very day she returned, in June, the same horse cut its foot and was lame for a fortnight. Later it caught a cold, and this time, instead of recovering, the animal grew more and more feeble and on 16 September it died.

At this point Mr Ettrick had no reason to suspect witchcraft – he blamed the vet who had treated his horse. However, he soon began to have his doubts. Four days after his horse died, one of his pigs fell ill and had to be slaughtered. His dog also died. There seemed to be no reason for these illnesses, and all medication failed to have any beneficial effect whatsoever. A horse he borrowed from a neighbour also grew weak. And more seriously, his children became ill, particularly the youngest one.

This child, a boy, was born on 22 July 1804. Susan Woodrow acted as a nurse at the birth. She was the first to hold the baby who,

17

according to the diary, was in pain and torment from the day he was born. For four wretched months, Ettrick watched over his son each sleepless, restless night, and as he sat beside the poor infant, he began to link the different happenings together. By 4 November he was sufficiently convinced that there was evil afoot to write of his suspicions in his diary.

Ettrick sent Susan away from the house. He also acquired for his baby son a charm, a phylactery consisting of 'sacred words' inscribed in an ancient script on a piece of parchment and contained in a tiny box which he strapped to the child's body. This in itself is an indication of how strongly this man of the cloth now believed in the power of witchcraft. Apparently it worked and happily the baby grew strong and well.

For some reason, although he suspected Susan to be the cause of all that had happened, Ettrick allowed her back to the vicarage some weeks later to carry out various household tasks. Immediately, his son grew ill again. And yet, instead of dismissing her straight away, the vicar allowed her to stay. One can only think that he was by now so convinced of Susan's powers that he was afraid to upset her. In his diary of 1 December, he directly accuses her of witchcraft. She seemed to be glad, he said, when the child suffered, and never once expressed any hopes that the little boy would get better. He made up his mind to dismiss her but put off doing so until January, obviously worried about confronting her.

How long he would have allowed her to stay is impossible to say, even though his child was suffering. What seems to have persuaded him to act is a disturbing dream which finally shook him out of his indecision. In the dream, a strange black bird flew into his room, and after flying round him several times, landed on his head. He pulled it off, and after something of a struggle, wrung its neck and threw it to the floor. His cat, transfixed by all this, refused to go near the dead bird. Whatever the significance of this dream, it finally persuaded Ettrick to send Susan away for good. She, for her part, tried one more time to come back, arriving at the house with some letters from a neighbour which she had offered to deliver. Ettrick refused either to

RIGHT '. . . a strange black bird flew into his room.'

18

accept the letters or allow her into the vicarage, and with great reluctance Susan eventually turned and walked away for ever.

After that, William Ettrick's young son recovered and the family's misfortunes ended. Ettrick listed the 'Works of Susan' including the illness of his family and the deaths of the animals, and mentioning also that the part of the garden tended by Susan had a succession of crop failures, that potatoes stored by her turned bad, and that bees looked after by her left the hives. He knew he didn't have enough evidence against her to take her to court, her 'crimes' being all 'works of darkness'.

Was he right? Was Susan Woodrow in possession of strange powers, or was it all a series of unhappy coincidences? Had his position as a clergyman attracted the curse of evil forces, or was he simply blaming her for his family's bad luck? The Reverend William Ettrick, sensible, intelligent, well-educated, was quite adamant. As he wrote in his diary: 'I was once incredulous about the power of witchcraft, but have no doubts remaining.'

RIGHT **A distant view of St Catherine's Chapel near Abbotsbury, Dorset.**

Chesil Beach

Having curved around Lyme Bay, the Dorset coastline runs smooth and clean from Eype by Bridport south east towards Portland. At Abbotsbury it wavers, and the hills fall away from Blackdown with that curious suddenness which makes the cattle in the soft fields by the water's edge look slightly incongruous. But though the coastline now dips in and out, the beach continues straight and true, for all the world as if a child, asked to mark it on a map, has grown tired of

RIGHT **Chesil Beach.**

ABOVE **West Bay at the western end of Chesil Beach.**

accuracy and simply drawn a line from A to B. This is Chesil Beach, one of Nature's strangest whims. Twenty miles long in all, this last stretch is a great bank of pebbles, holding back the sea on one side, trapping a lake on the other.

In 1740, Chesil was lashed by a terrible storm which lasted for two weeks and eventually drove the treasure ship *Hope* of Amsterdam onto the beach where she broke up, spilling out her cargo of gold and silver and precious jewels. Not surprisingly, hordes of people came from Weymouth and Portland to try to recover the riches, and their frenzied greed led to riots. The weather was so appalling that some died of exposure as they dug among the pebbles, but no-one seems to have been injured in the fighting. Eventually, calm was restored and the ship's owners were able to retrieve thirty thousand pounds worth of treasure – although nearly as much again was by that time lining the pockets of the local inhabitants.

Chesil Beach rises as high as fifty feet, and shelves sharply into the sea, and the *Hope* was by no means the only ship to founder here. Spanish galleons lie below the water, and rusty cannon, hastily jettisoned by anxious crews in an attempt to lighten the load and prevent their vessels being driven onto the shore by wind and tide. There is an official war grave, too, the submarine M1, her hatches sealed and her ill-fated crew within her still. Nelson's flag captain, Admiral Sir Thomas Hardy, whose lonely monument stands high up on nearby Blackdown, called this place Dead Man's Bay with justification.

The bold sweep of pebbles that could be so dangerous to ships nevertheless protected the stretch of water behind it, and the land behind that. But even Chesil Beach is fallible. One black night in 1824 the sea swept in, flooding the fields to a depth of twenty feet and decimating the village of Fleet. The parish church was particularly badly hit – all but the chancel was destroyed.

As you walk along the beach, you cannot help but be aware that this is no ordinary place. Sometimes on a calm day, as the anglers silently fish for conger and bass, there is an almost oppressive quietness, broken only by the sound of the pebbles beneath your feet. These seem to have been graded according to size, the larger ones at the Portland end of the beach. They say you can tell exactly which part of the beach you're on just by the size of the pebbles. They're beautiful pebbles, too, pink, grey, blue, green and tan, some marbled with thin veins of colour, all worn smooth and round by countless tides. Except for the holy stones, the so-called hag-stones. These are much more clumsily fashioned, buff coloured with cream and grey markings, and a hole running through them. They are regarded as lucky charms, and fishermen tied them to the gunwales of their boats to ward off witches, for sometimes while others hauled in nets full of fish, one boat would fail to catch anything and the fishermen would know it had been bewitched.

In his classic adventure story *Moonfleet,* J. Meade Falkner wrote of 'a lake of brackish water . . . such a place as they call in the Indies a lagoon, being shut off from the open Channel by a monstrous great beach or dyke of pebbles'. This is Chesil – Moonfleet is a corruption of Mohun Fleet, the Mohuns being a powerful family around here once. It's not surprising that Falkner chose to use this strange place as the setting for his story, nor is it surprising that there is a story about the very existence of Chesil Beach itself, for how else can you explain this puzzling addition to the Dorset coastline, this extraordinary after-thought.

Once again, a mighty storm plays its part, for it seems that round about 1500 a buccaneer, fleeing from the King's ships, was forced to take shelter at Abbotsbury. The storm raged all night, and by morning a whole new beach had taken shape, trapping the buccaneer. Good fortune was on his side, however, for he was able to hide his booty in a nearby church yard and made his escape. The King's ships were powerless. Chesil Beach, washed up in a single night, kept them out at sea.

Moving Stones

On the heath at Studland, overlooking the sea and Poole Harbour, is a huge rock made of iron-impregnated sandstone. Eighteen feet high, eighty feet in circumference and weighing about four hundred tons, it is an imposing sight. Geologists will tell you that it is a fragment of the thick layer of sandstone which covered this area ages ago, weathered into shape by the elements and the passing of time. What a dull explanation. How much more colourful to listen to the folklore which tells how the Devil, stalking across the Isle of Wight, stood on the Needles and with a mighty swing of his arm, flung this huge stone at Corfe Castle ... or Bindon Abbey ... or was it at the spire of Salisbury Cathedral. Whatever his target, he missed, and the Agglestone has lain on the Heath ever since.

Also known as the Devil's Anvil because of its shape, there are several interpretations of the name Agglestone. Possibly it derives from the old English word *Hagolstan* or hailstone, which certainly supports the idea that it fell from heaven, although the word is older than Corfe Castle, the presumed target. On the other hand, *halig* means holy, and it's quite possible that offerings of some sort were made here. The stone would undoubtedly have formed an impressive altar. A third suggestion uses the local meaning of the word aggle, which is to wobble, or wobbly. Picture an eight year old with an aggle tooth and you'll know exactly what I mean. They used to say that if you knew precisely where and how to push, it was possible to make the huge Agglestone rock to and fro, despite its immense size and weight. However, in 1970, the Devil's Anvil slipped over onto its side, aggled, no doubt, just once too often.

The Devil, apparently, was given to flinging huge chunks of rock about the place, sometimes in anger, but also in play. Quoits was his game, pitching a ring over a pin set in the ground. On the downs between Portesham Hill and the Hardy Monument there's a group of

27

stones which are said to have been thrown by the Devil during a game of quoits on Portland.

These are called collectively the Hellstone – once again overtones of hailstone and things falling from the sky. The other explanation for them is that they form a Neolithic burial chamber dating from about 3,000 BC. It would originally have been covered by a mound of earth about ninety feet long, but time has taken its toll. Over the years some of the supporting stones sank into the ground and the great capstone slid off, coming to rest at a rakish angle. In the 1860s the Reverend Martin Tupper took it upon himself to restore the Hellstone to its former glory and set about rebuilding it. A team of eight Portland quarrymen, using screwjacks, managed to raise the oval capstone back on to the nine newly-righted supporting pillars. It was a task that called for great skill and expert judgment, for it must weigh sixteen tons, but happily they were successful, as you can see to this day.

When the good people of Dorset were not dodging mighty boulders hurled by the Devil, they had to watch out for the giants. Giants too enjoyed a bit of stone throwing – they say that's how the huge rock at Brockhampton Green came to be there. Two other giants, determined to establish once and for all who was the stronger, agreed to settle their dispute with a stone-throwing competition. Standing on Norden Hill, they aimed at Hanging, or Henning, Hill across the valley. The first giant managed a respectable distance, but the second giant's stone fell so short he flew into a rage, and died of

LEFT **Felicity Young, Cornish-based painter, who has done ten of the drawings, especially commissioned for 'Legends of Dorset'. A water colourist, her paintings grow from sketches, notes and photographs taken on location. She has done illustrations for Bossiney titles on Devon, Cornwall, Somerset, Avon and now Dorset. Educated at Lord Digby's Grammar School, Sherborne, Felicity says: 'I feel Dorset is a county so full of legend that the artist's imagination is easily fired by tales of ghostly happenings and by the intriguing characters who have lived here. You cannot fail to be affected by the sense of mystery which surrounds the beautiful landscape'.**

ABOVE **Hellstone: '. . . overtones of hailstones and things falling from the sky.'**

vexation. His grave, a long mound, is at Cheselbourne, and nearby stand two large stones, reminders of the giants themselves.

These two stones are also part of another phenomenon not unheard of in Dorset, for it is said that when the cocks crow in Cheselbourne, these stones move. And they are by no means the only stones capable of going walk-about. On the road west of Weymouth, at Langton Cross by the turning to Langton Herring, there's a stone, possibly a boundary marker, which according to tradition each New Year's Eve walks down to the Fleet and Chesil Beach, dips its head in the water and then goes back. And the wishing stone at Bettiscombe rolls down Sliding Hill on Midsummer's Eve and returns the following day. The idea of impassive hunks of rock lumbering around the countryside is so delightful it seems churlish to point out that those two dates in the calendar are usually marked by the sort of celebrations which leave the senses – and witnesses – a little less reliable than usual.

Furthermore, whilst we're on the subject of moving stones, in certain parts of Dorset whole churches have uprooted themselves and settled elsewhere. At least, the foundations of these churches have moved. When the church at West Dawlish burnt down at the end of the sixteenth century, the villagers tried to rebuild it. But the work they did each day was undone each night and eventually they abandoned the project. At Folke, a tiny village near Sherborne, they started to build a church in Broke Wood, but as they did so it was moved, again at night, to its present site about a mile away. The same thing happened at Holnest.

And at Winterbourne Whitechurch, Round Meadow was chosen as the place to build a new church. Now this meadow was believed to be cursed because a farmer had once cut it on a Sunday, and no crops would grow in it. Before too long the villagers came to the conclusion that the curse was affecting the church too, because each morning when they arrived to start work, they found the stones they had laid the day before had moved to another field. Like the people of West Dawlish, they knew when to give in gracefully. A different site was chosen, and work went ahead uninterrupted until the fine new church was completed.

KING CHARLES II
ESCAPED CAPTURE THROUGH THIS LANE
SEP^R XXIII, MDCLI.

WHEN MIDST YOUR FIERCEST FOES ON EVERY SIDE
FOR YOUR ESCAPE GOD DID A LANE PROVIDE.
(THOMAS FULLERS WORTHIES)

ERECTED SEP^R XXIII MDCCCCI.

A.M.B.

Famous Characters I

Judge Jeffreys

What is it that makes certain people stand out in the crowd? Why do some become a talking point while others pass by unremarked? These chosen few enjoy more than a brief moment of notoriety, more than a sudden rise to fame before sinking into obscurity. Not merely local heroes, they leave their mark on an entire nation, and though the details may not be remembered, their names are not forgotten. The reason is quite simply that they are larger than life, more dangerous, more honourable or more charismatic than the rest. Dorset has its share of legendary characters, amongst them the cruel and merciless Judge Jeffreys whose ruthless brutality cut down those supporters of the Monmouth Rebellion who survived the Battle of Sedgemoor; the Tolpuddle Martyrs whose fight for better working conditions laid the foundations for today's trades union movement; and Lillie Langtry, the woman who won not only the heart of the Prince of Wales, but also the adulation of the country.

Judge George Jeffreys was the man who led the aptly-named Bloody Assizes on behalf of King James II at a time when England was still trying to regain its composure after the Civil War. The line of succession to the throne was less than straightforward, Protestants and Catholics viewed each other with grave distrust and there was the ever present threat of intervention from the Continent.

When Charles II, who had been restored as monarch following the interregnum, died he was succeeded by his brother the Duke of York, who duly became James II. At first he was regarded as a popular king but nevertheless a revolt was soon launched against him. This was led by James, Duke of Monmouth, the illegitimate son of Charles

LEFT **A stone recalling King Charles II escaping capture through this Dorset lane.**

33

II, who landed at Lyme Regis with a band of about eighty followers and marched to Taunton, gathering support as he went. Eventually Monmouth clashed with the King's army, led by Feversham, at the Battle of Sedgemoor on 6 July 1685 – the last battle fought on English soil. Dubbed the Pitchfork Rebellion, most of the rebels were country men from Dorset and Somerset and were little match for Feversham's well-trained soldiers. Many of them died that day. Monmouth himself was found hiding in a ditch and although he sought mercy from James II he was executed on Tower Hill for treason. For some time, however, rumours persisted among his loyal followers that the Duke had escaped and hopes were long cherished that he would return one day to lead them to victory, like a Jacobean El Cid.

Although the uprising had been thoroughly quashed, James wanted to discourage any further thoughts of rebellion. And so he decided to punish all those found guilty of supporting the Duke of Monmouth. This in itself was a harsh decision; even Cromwell had only tried the officers of the Royalist army, sparing the ordinary soldiers. Even more harsh was his choice of judge.

George Jeffreys was born in Denbighshire but educated at St Paul's Free School in London. Keen-witted and ambitious, he saw that there was money to be made in the legal profession and determined to make it his career. He entered the Inner Temple, one of the chief Inns of Court, and by the age of twenty had been called to the Bar. He married well – a young widow who just happened to be the daughter of an alderman of the city of London – and soon rose to prominence. He caught the attention of the King – Charles II was still on the throne – gained the Recordership of the city of London and became not only a judge but also a lord.

However, he allowed ambition to scar his undoubted ability and earned a reputation for ruthlessness and lack of mercy. He was 37 when James II sent him to deal with the rebels and already he was regarded as aggressive, overbearing and arrogant.

LEFT **The Sedgemoor memorial stone – the last battle fought on English soil, where many Dorset men went in support of the Duke of Monmouth who had landed at Lyme Regis.**

As Judge Jeffreys travelled from court to court – Winchester, Taunton and Dorchester were the most significant – it soon became apparent why these were called the Bloody Assizes. Some 1400 prisoners were brought before him, 300 were hanged and 800 were sold as slaves to the colonies. Some were given as gifts to courtiers to sell for their own profit. The hearings were a mockery. Jeffreys dealt with each case so swiftly it was impossible for the trials to be fair. In order to speed up the proceedings, he hinted that pleas of 'guilty' would be treated mercifully – 'not guilty' pleas took longer to deal with. But it was a cruel trick; the hapless rebels received no compassion.

One contemporary writer described 'unheard of cruelties and barbarous proceedings . . . whippings and cruel imprisonments, and the most exquisite tortures which none could invent or inflict but your Lordship who is supposed by all to have a heart of marble and entrails of brass.'

Not content with a straightforward death penalty, Jeffreys insisted that his victims were hung, drawn and quartered so that there were 'men hung all up and down the towns of the county, and their heads and quarter scattered up and down the highways and publick places'.

Returning to London, Jeffreys' days were numbered. Corrupt, greedy, ruthless, he was increasingly hated. He was safe only as long as he had the support of the King, but James II had also fallen from grace and was forced to flee the country. Jeffreys realised he, too, needed to escape and disguising himself, made elaborate plans. But he was caught and, followed by an angry mob, taken to the Tower. With half of London baying for his blood, Fate was kinder to him than he had been to the countless men and women who suffered his rough justice. Judge George Jeffreys died in his cell, aged forty, before he came to trial.

Judge Jeffreys' time in Dorchester was spent at the Oak Room in the Antelope Hotel. At the time it was the only room in town large enough to hold the trials, an oak-panelled room still used today but for happier occasions. Jeffreys stayed in rooms nearby and made his

RIGHT **The Hangman's Cottage, Dorchester.**

ABOVE **Judge Jeffreys's Court at the Antelope Hotel, Dorchester.**

way to the Antelope Hotel by a secret passage so that the angry crowds would not see him.

The Bloody Assizes opened there on 5 September 1685 and 340 prisoners came before the judge. By the time the court moved on, Jeffreys had sentenced 74 men to death, condemned 175 to transportation and pardoned 55. The rest were remanded in custody or set free for lack of evidence.

These days the Antelope Hotel is part of a pedestrianised shopping area. The streets are busy, the pub is crowded. Standing amid the everyday bustle, it is strange to remember the cruelty that took place here, to imagine the fear with which men entered the Oak Room, and the despair with which they left, to picture the crowds who must have witnessed all this. It is not difficult to forget the twentieth century for a few moments, and shiver at the thought of those dark days when the Hanging Judge brought the Bloody Assizes to Dorchester.

Famous Characters II

Tolpuddle Martyrs

A century and a half after Judge Jeffreys held his Bloody Assizes, six Dorset men found themselves on the receiving end of injustice, helpless against those who abuse power and privilege. But unlike those unfortunate people who were sentenced by the Judge, whose names have been forgotten now, these men became the focus of a nationwide campaign and in their way, helped change the course of history. They were the Tolpuddle Martyrs.

This band of six were farm labourers who, like workers the length and breadth of the country, found their working conditions becoming increasingly intolerable. In 1795 something called the Speenhamland System effectively saw that agricultural workers were paid pitiably low wages, supplemented by meagre poor relief funds when it was deemed necessary. Poor relief was administered by the local landowner, squire and parson – not only could they set the wages as low as they liked, they also decided who should receive financial help. It was obviously unwise to upset them. Furthermore, the Enclosure Acts had resulted in acres of common land becoming private property. The workers grew poorer and more desperate; the landowners grew richer and more powerful.

The law arrests the man or woman
Who steals the goose from off the common,
But leaves the greater rascal loose,
Who steals the common from the goose.

By the 1830s, Trades Union movements had started to form in London and the more industrialised north. In Tolpuddle, in the heart of agricultural Dorset, the farm workers had tried to protest against their low wages, a complaint answered swiftly by their employers who promptly cut their money from nine shillings a week to seven shillings.

And so, in October 1833, George Loveless, self-educated and a Methodist preacher, started a Friendly Society of Agricultural Labourers. Meetings were held at Thomas Standfield's cottage, and there were six members – Thomas and his son John, George Loveless and his brother James, James Hammett and James Brine. Their aim was to unite in their fight for better pay and to put an end to the injustices which abounded. The society, however, was to be short lived. Before the year was out, they had been betrayed.

A labourer called Edward Legg asked to join the new society and was duly sworn in. Trade unions were by this time perfectly legal, but the tradition of pledging an oath of loyalty still lingered on from earlier days. It proved to be their downfall. Legg was a spy supplying information to the magistrates and farmers who regarded Loveless and his friends as trouble–makers, and saw the formation of a friendly society as insurrection. On Legg's evidence, the six were arrested and charged with participating 'in the administration of an illegal oath'. Naturally, they were found guilty.

Two days before the six men were arrested, notices were posted around the area by the justices warning that 'mischievous and designing persons' were trying to persuade workers to join societies and swear unlawful oaths of loyalty. 'Any person who shall become a member of such a society, or take an oath or consent to any test to declaration not authorised by law will become guilty of a felony and liable to be transported for seven years.'

George Loveless had read one of these notices, and had put it in his pocket. It was found on him when he was arrested and used as proof that he had knowingly broken the law. It was useless for him to protest that the Tolpuddle Friendly Society had been formed weeks before the notices were posted.

The justices were determined to make an example of the six farm workers, to deal with them severely in order to discourage others from challenging the system. The court found the men guilty of sedition and illegal procedures. Taken from Dorchester jail to the prison hulks at Portsmouth, they were later moved to Plymouth and on 11 April 1834 five of them were transported to New South Wales

RIGHT **Martyrs' tree at Tolpuddle.**

ABOVE RIGHT **Ancient punishment at Pimperne: site of the last pillorying in Dorset.**

ABOVE **This photograph shows the area worn by the prisoners' feet when held in the stocks.**

on the convict ship *Surrey*. George himself fell ill, and he sailed on a later ship, the *William Metcalfe* which took him to Tasmania.

Conditions for convicts were appalling to say the least, overcrowded and filthy. The men were kept in chains the whole time, and punishments included the use of branding irons and the cat o'nine tails. Some of the other convicts were violent and hardened criminals, desperate men with quite literally nothing to lose; others, like the men from Tolpuddle, were wretched creatures sentenced to transportation for pathetically minor offences. When the *Surrey* arrived in Australia, four of the friends were put on a chain gang. The fifth, James Hammett, was sold for £1 and made to walk 400 miles to his new place of work. George Loveless, landing in Tasmania in October, was slightly luckier: he fared as well as any one could under the circumstances.

And there the story may well have ended, the men from Dorset

forgotten on the other side of the world. But back in Britain, attitudes were changing. People of influence were beginning to see the injustice around them. The voice of the union movement was making itself heard – and those in power were forced to listen. There was a wave of protest over the arrest and conviction of the Tolpuddle Martyrs, protest that grew in size and strength. Supporters such as Robert Owen, a wealthy manufacturer who was one of the first Socialists, fought for a pardon for the six men. A petition was sent to the Home Secretary, Lord Melbourne, who rejected it. Undeterred, the protest continued. Melbourne became Prime Minister again, and a more amenable man, Lord John Russell, took over as Home Secretary. Thomas Wakley, editor of the *Lancet,* took up the issue in Parliament and refused to let it drop. It was Wakley who showed Russell the 80,000 signatures on the petition, convincing him both of the strength of public opinion, and of the injustice of the sentences

and the trial itself. Eventually Russell was able to persuade
Melbourne who in turn approached the King. In March 1836, two
years after the trial, the King granted all six men a Royal Pardon.

It took time to bring them home. It was September 1837 before
they returned to Plymouth as national heroes. There was a reception
at the Antelope Hotel at Dorchester – strange that it should feature
again in Dorset's history – and the following Easter Monday, they
marched in a procession through London.

When the excitement had all died down, the men found work in
Essex, and in 1844 they decided to emigrate to Canada and make a
new start for themselves and their families. James Hammett was the

LEFT **Gravestone of James Hammett, Tolpuddle martyr and pioneer of trades unionism.**

exception; he had taken rather longer to return to England and he chose instead to go back to Tolpuddle.

Today in Tolpuddle, you can sit beneath the tree on the village green where the men met and talked, and you can still see Thomas Standfield's cottage where the Society was founded. In 1934, the TUC built a row of cottages in memory of the Martyrs, as well as a small museum which traces the history of the trades union movement. It's visited by unionists not only from this country but from around the world, as the Visitors' Book records. For the foundations of the union movement were laid by men just like George Loveless and his friends, honest ordinary men who wanted the right to earn a decent living for themselves and their families, men who stood up against people infinitely stronger and more powerful in order to fight for their beliefs and win dignity and respect for working men. In St John's churchyard, in this small village in the heart of Dorset, the inscription on James Hammett's gravestone tells the whole story:

James Hammett
Tolpuddle Martyr, Pioneer of Trades Unionism,
Champion of Freedom.

Famous Characters III

Lillie Langtry: A Legendary Mistress

On a more frivolous note, let me tell you about another of Dorset's legendary characters, a beautiful woman who came to live in a fine house in Bournemouth in the late 1870s. On reflection, to describe her as frivolous is perhaps to underestimate her, for in her own way she fought for freedom and independence for women at a time when women in general were regarded as second-class citizens without an original thought in their heads, and wives in particular were little more than chattels belonging to their husbands. This woman captivated London society, sparked off fashion trends followed by shop girls and chic hostesses alike, and stole the heart of the future King of England. She was Lillie Langtry, mistress of Bertie, then the Prince of Wales, later Edward VII.

Lillie was born in Jersey in 1853, tomboy sister to six brothers and daughter of William Corbet le Breton, Dean of Jersey and himself something of a womaniser. Lillie became famous for her beauty at a very early age and when she reached twenty she married a young – and wealthy – Irish landowner called Edward Langtry. He took her to live in London, in Eaton Square, and it was not long before Lillie was welcomed into society circles. She was one of those rare creatures, a social butterfly whose attraction lasts, and she was soon established as one of the most charismatic and popular women of her time. Lillie blossomed, but her poor husband did not really take to life in London, and began spending more and more time in the country, leaving his wife to enjoy herself.

RIGHT **Lillie Langtry, a legendary mistress. Entitled 'A Jersey Lily', painted by John Everey Millais, this was Lillie's favourite portrait of herself.**

46

Lillie became, in effect, a professional beauty. Millais painted her, as did the other great artists of the day, and postcards of her portrait made her famous throughout the land. Women everywhere watched avidly her style of dress, the colours she chose to wear, the way she did her hair, and they tried to copy her. But there was more to Lillie than good looks. There was also an almost indefinable quality about her that added something to people's perception of her. Men and women fell under her spell. Daisy, Countess of Warwick, wrote of her: 'She had dewy violet eyes, a complexion like a peach. How can words convey the vitality, the glow, the amazing charm that made this fascinating woman the centre of any group she entered?'

Not surprisingly, the Prince of Wales also fell for Lillie. Bertie, sentenced to a life of privileged idleness, had already indulged in various flirtations, but this was known only to a few people. With Lillie it was different. Having engineered a meeting with her at a specially arranged dinner party, he was soon seeing her regularly, and more significantly, being seen with her. He was enchanted by her beauty, her charm and her independence of spirit. Lillie treated him as an equal; the Prince of Wales, used to ingratiating deference, found this irresistible. Lillie became his acknowledged mistress.

It has to be remembered that this was a time when hypocrisy reigned. The image of Victorian family life, upright, moral, united, often belied the true picture of husband and wife living more or less separate lives. Appearances were everything, and as long as certain rules of discretion were followed, life continued on an even keel. It was an arrangement that in many cases suited both parties. It was also a time when royalty lived free from the glare of publicity and speculation that follows their every move these days. Although the upper echelons of society knew what was going on, the vast majority of people in the country would have been completely unaware of the nature of Bertie's liaison with Lillie. Consequently, the two were able to spend a great deal of time together.

What is remarkable, however, is that Lillie became a good friend of Bertie's wife, the gentle Alexandra, a friendship that continued

after Bertie died. She was even presented to Queen Victoria, and in her own inimitable style could not resist wearing in her hair three ostrich feathers, the Prince of Wales' own emblem.

The Prince decided that he and Lillie needed a retreat away from London, and so he built her a house in Bournemouth, up on the cliffs among the pine trees, a half-timbered brick building surrounded by lawns and gardens. It's a delightful house, large but not ostentatious, welcoming and comfortable. Lillie named it The Red House and it still bears the little touches that she gave it to make it her own. There are strange inscriptions on the walls: *Dulce Domum* – sweet home – it says on a south facing wall, and inside in the entrance hall 'And yours my friend'. The dining hall with its minstrels' gallery has painted on one wall 'They say – what say they? Let them say', Lillie's view on gossip perhaps. In several places you can see the initials 'ELL' inscribed – on one of the downstairs windows they have been cut into the glass together with two hearts and the date 1883.

The Prince's room is at the front of the house, spacious and comfortable with French windows opening onto a balcony. It has an enormous four-poster bed, and an inglenook fireplace decorated with blue Delft tiles depicting scenes from Shakespeare's plays. Like the

49

ABOVE **The King's Room at the Langtry Manor Hotel, Bournemouth.**

rest of the house, it has the sure touch of a woman with good taste, an instinct for home-making and the money to pay for it. Across the landing from Bertie's room is a small hatch through which he could spy on the dining room below, to see who else was there before deciding whether or not to put in an appearance himself.

Lillie and the Prince of Wales had ten years together, but eventually he fell for someone else. He'd always had a roving eye and Lillie, too, was something of a free spirit. During that time together, she gave birth to a baby daughter, fathered by Bertie's cousin Prince Louis of Battenberg. After Bertie moved on, Lillie embarked upon a stage career, first as an actress, later as a theatre company manager, something she did with typical verve and success. The Prince remained her friend, and wrote to her for many years. Lillie went to America and acquired a millionaire admirer willing to take care of her financial as well as her emotional needs. Several other wealthy lovers followed. Her first husband, whom she had divorced, died in an asylum in 1897. In 1899 Lillie married again and became Lady de Bathe, wife of Sir Hugo de Bathe, a man several years her junior.

Lillie Langtry was a remarkable woman who led a remarkable life. Oscar Wilde wrote of her: 'She is the most beautiful woman in the world. She stood for the right of women to lead an independent, unshackled life.' The Red House is now an hotel, the Langtry Manor Hotel, filled with mementoes and souvenirs of Lillie – paintings, photographs, newspaper cuttings, theatre bills, even some of her dresses.

Lillie died in 1929 at the age of 75, thirteen years after her prince. She spent the last years of her life in Monaco, but the sunny house in Derby Road still seems to echo with the laughter and the happiness and the love that the Prince of Wales, the man born to be King of England, shared with his beautiful mistress Lillie Langtry.

Murders I

Royal Murder

Even a county as pretty as Dorset has had its darker moments and down the ages passion, greed and outright evil have led to murder. The stories of some of the more infamous cases live on today.

One of the best known stories happened more than a thousand years ago in Corfe, before the castle whose ruins now point accusingly towards the sky was even built. The year was 978 AD and Edward had been crowned King of Wessex and All England, three years earlier at the age of fifteen. He had come to the throne following the death of his father Edgar. In many respects Edward was a popular king, but some factions would have preferred his younger step-brother Ethelred as their monarch. The old King had instituted some strict and unwelcome reforms; Edward, it was felt, was quite likely to continue along the same path. Consequently, he had several enemies, some of them, such as the Earl of Mercia, powerful men. He had also to contend with the ambitions of his stepmother Elfrida.

Edward's brief reign lasted just three years, and ended that fateful day at Corfe. The young King had been hunting at Purbeck and decided to visit Ethelred. He was fond of his stepbrother and looked forward to seeing him. However, it was Elfrida who greeted him at the gate of the Saxon hunting lodge and offered him some wine. As he leaned forward unawares to take the goblet, his stepmother stabbed him. In the confusion, his horse bolted. Edward, wounded and bleeding, slipped from his saddle but caught his foot in the stirrup and was draggeed along the ground. Elfrida ordered her men to go after him; by the time they caught up with him, Edward was dead.

LEFT **Corfe Castle dramatically captured by photographer Rob Scott.**

ABOVE **The castle seen from the village below.**

RIGHT **Royal Murder: 'In the confusion his horse bolted . . .'**

Elfrida was anxious that the body should be hidden. She was determined nothing should stand in the way of her plans to have Ethelred crowned. The dead King was taken to the house of an old blind lady and shortly afterwards Elfrida's men threw the body down a well, hoping it would never be found. However, a year later the body was recovered and carried to St Mary's Church at Wareham, to be buried in what is now known as the St Edward Chapel. The following year, the body was moved again, this time to Shaftesbury Abbey, and Edward was canonised as a martyr by the Pope.

Conspiracy and treason are common enough factors in English history, particularly in those early days before the country was properly united and when usurpers from overseas regularly invaded our shores. The King who died peacefully in his own bed was lucky indeed. Edward's demise could so easily have been marked down as

just another chapter in the story of Britain, and forgotten completely, but for the legends associated with it that are still told in Dorset today.

The first concerns the blind lady whose house was used as a hiding place for the King's body. It's said that a mysterious light filled the cottage that night at midnight, and that the old lady's sight was restored. Naturally, she was delighted and later when the King's tomb at Shaftesbury became a place of pilgrimage she determined to visit it each year, taking with her sprigs of white broom, the first flower she had seen after the miracle. Along the route she followed, seeds fell and now white broom lines the way. It is known locally as Martyr's Broom.

Secondly, the King's body, having lain for a whole year in the well, was finally discovered when a brilliant ray of light illuminated the spot. The body was absolutely intact, and the water had remained completely pure. This was taken as a sign that the water had healing

LEFT **Wareham: A year later the body was recovered and carried to Wareham.**

properties, and the well became a shrine known as St Edward's fountain, visited by the sick and infirm hoping for a cure.

Edward's stepbrother Ethelred, incidentally, ruled for 37 years, a reign that saw the return of the Danes. He married a Norman princess, which some say opened the way for the Norman Conquest exactly fifty years after his death. He was dubbed Ethelred the Unraed, a term which really translates as the 'ill-advised' but lives on in people's memories as Ethelred the Unready. Edward, the young murdered King, became St Edward the Martyr, and pilgrims journeyed to his shrine at Shaftesbury Abbey until his bones were lost in the Dissolution of the Monasteries in the sixteenth century. Had he lived, he may well have been a strict and uncompromising ruler like his father before him, but his early death ensured instead that he lives on in people's memories as a Good King. Such is the fickleness of history that legend and hearsay leave a much greater impression than fact.

Murders II
Jack the Ripper and Dorset

The town of Wimborne Minster exudes an air of calm orderliness. Its buildings are a happy mix of old and very old, the few modern additions blending in well. The whole town is dominated by the speckled grey and brown stone Minster which gives the place its name. The original town square, the Cornmarket, is home to the annual Folk Festival; another open space, 'The Square', was created when a ruined medieval church was demolished at the beginning of the nineteenth century. An old coaching inn, the King's Head Hotel, with a fine coaching arch, stands on the west side of it. Its façade was reconstructed following a fire in the 1880s, not long after the building on the north side which houses Lloyd's Bank, was completed. It is easy to picture Wimborne in those days, respectable and safe.

Contrast it with London's East End in Victorian times. Crowded, dirty, dangerous, populated by thieves and whores and drunkards, it was an area that offered little that was honest and decent. The two places could hardly have less in common. They might as well have been on different planets.

And yet there is a macabre link between the two, for buried in the cemetery at Wimborne is a man who may have been the notorious Jack the Ripper.

The murders of five prostitutes in the autumn of 1888 are among the most famous in criminal history. The area around Spitalfields market was home to London's unfortunates and inadequates and life was cheap but these murders were particularly horrific and terrified even those used to violence. The victims were all women of easy

RIGHT **Felicity Young's impression of a 'Jack the Ripper' murder.**

virtue, well known on the streets and in the pubs. In each case, there was no sign of a struggle, suggesting that the women knew their attacker, or at least had no reason to be afraid of him until it was too late. There was no evidence of sexual assault, or rather no evidence that was made public at the time. But the most nauseating feature of the murders was the terrible mutilation of the bodies.

The women's throats were slit, their faces slashed, and with one exception, they were disembowelled. The fifth and final victim, Mary Jane Kelly, was murdered in her bed, her head almost severed from her body, her heart and kidneys laid out on a table beside the bed, her intestines hung from picture hooks on the wall. The Ripper worked swiftly, with awesome ferocity. The hideous details of his attacks, the evidence of the witnesses, the reports of the police officers trying to find the murderer have intrigued 'Ripperologists' ever since, and inspired many theories, expounded in books and articles. But the fact remains that no-one has ever proved conclusively the identity of Jack the Ripper.

Several names have been suggested and in each case there is a certain amount of evidence to corroborate the idea. Peter Underwood, in his book *Jack the Ripper: 100 Years of Mystery* published to mark the centenary of the murders, chronicles the different schools of thought in far greater detail than is possible here. Suffice it to say that a strong contender is a man called Montague John Druitt.

Druitt's father, William, was a doctor in Wimborne and one of the town's most respected citizens. Montague went to Winchester College and New College, Oxford, before being admitted to the Inner Temple in 1882. He was called to the Bar three years later shortly before his father died. However, there is no record of him ever accepting a brief, and in 1888 he worked as an assistant teacher at a private school in Blackheath. Things began to go wrong for him. He was dismissed from the school, his mother became insane in July of that year, a month or so before the first murder, and Druitt feared that he himself was going mad. At the end of the year he drowned himself in the Thames. There were no more Ripper murders after that.

LEFT **Could this be the grave of Jack the Ripper?**

There are several reasons why Druitt is a suspect. Because of the nature of the atrocities carried out on the women's bodies, it is assumed that the murderer had some knowledge of anatomy, a doctor perhaps. Druitt was not a doctor himself, but his father, his uncle and his cousin all were. The Ripper would very probably have been left-handed – Druitt was ambidextrous. His cousin Lionel had a surgery of sorts in the Minories, an area just a short distance from the sites of the murders.

Sir Melville Macnaghten, who joined Scotland Yard as an Assistant Chief Constable in 1889, believed Druitt was the murderer. He wrote: '... from private information I have little doubt but that his own family suspected this man of being the Whitechapel murderer.' It was alleged that he was 'sexually insane'. Major Arthur Griffiths, Inspector of Prisons, wrote in 1898, 'There is every reason to believe that his own friends entertained grave doubts about him.' Sir Charles Warren, Commissioner of Police at the time of the murders, believed the murderer to be a sex maniac who committed suicide; Sir John Moylan, Assistant Under Secretary at the Home Office, said: 'The murderer, it is now certain, escaped justice by committing suicide at the end of 1888.' And so the evidence goes on. There is even a possibility that Druitt's family killed him in order to put an end to the gruesome attacks.

The truth behind the awful murders may never be known. All the investigations by criminologists over the years have failed to produce conclusive proof. But Druitt was certainly one of the most likely suspects.

His body is buried in the cemetery on the outskirts of Wimborne, a simple cross marking his grave, the inscription giving only the barest detail of his life. The cemetery is neat and open, an avenue of manicured bushes leading up to the twin chapels, the wind blowing fresh and clean. Can it be that the man responsible for those sordid vicious deaths in the rancid alleyways of London's East End lies buried alongside the honest citizens who lived and died in Wimborne?

As yet, no-one can say for sure. But perhaps one day we'll know the truth about Jack the Ripper, and Montague John Druitt.

Murders III

'Cause Celebre' in Bournemouth

Murder is always headline news, but the circumstances of some murders capture public interest more than others. Crimes of passion, in particular, prompt strong feelings with popular opinion deciding well in advance of any judge or jury precisely who is guilty.

In Bournemouth in 1935 a murder was committed which had all the classic ingredients of a *cause celebre,* a real life story which was to live on in Terence Rattigan's play of that name. It was a drama with three characters: a talented vivacious woman, married to an older frail husband and in love with a young man scarcely more than a boy. It was a story that began in a quiet road in Dorset's premier seaside town and ended at the Old Bailey in London amid scenes of near-riot. Two of the characters were accused of murdering the third – one was found guilty by the court, the other committed suicide.

Manor Road is one of those sandy, pine-clad roads in Bournemouth close by the cliffs. Like a piano with its black and white keys, it is lined with old family houses whose large, lovingly tended gardens have been sold off to make room for new blocks of flats and modern hotels. Villa Madiera is one of the smaller old houses but nevertheless it is a charming place, cottagey almost, with a style and a character of its own. Looking at it today, comfortable, cosy even, it is hard to imagine it as the scene of a murder.

In 1935, the house was occupied by Francis and Alma Rattenbury. Francis was 67, a distinguished architect responsible for several fine buildings in Canada, but retired now, and sadly a little feeble in mind and body. His wife Alma was 30 years his junior, lively, intelligent, musical. She had been married before, and furthermore was a successful song writer. She published her songs under the name 'Lozanne', and one of them had been recorded by Peter Dawson. A woman of great personality, she had been awarded the *Croix de*

ABOVE **Villa Madiera in Manor Road,
Bournemouth: scene of a legendary murder.**

Guerre for her bravery at the front during the first World War. Alma
and Francis shared an affection and respect for each other, but he
couldn't match her vitality. After the birth of their son Peter, he told
her to live her own life.

George Stoner was a local lad, barely eighteen years of age, who
came to work for the Rattenburys as a chauffeur and handyman. At
first he cycled to and from the house each day, but soon Alma
suggested he should live in, so he moved into Villa Madiera in Manor
Road. And so the scene was set.

Alma Rattenbury was a woman in the prime of her life and very
beautiful. She was married to a man who needed a companion more
than he desired a wife. George, on the other hand, was young and
strong, naive and impressionable. Alma swept him off his feet. Before
long, they were lovers.

64

For a while a strange but convenient routine settled on the household. Alma was still fond of her husband – she called him 'Ratz' and spent her evenings playing cards with him. If he required her to be with him during the day, she was happy to do so. Otherwise she spent her time with George. Each night, she would kiss her husband goodnight, put Dinah the dog out into the garden, and retire to her room. George would invariably join her. Francis would stay in the drawing room for a while reading, then let Dinah back in and go to bed himself.

There was one other person in the household. Irene Riggs was employed as a companion and help, but she and Alma soon became good friends. Irene, the innocent bystander, was to find herself caught up in the events which followed, an integral part of the story which gripped the nation.

The evening of Sunday 24 March that year began much like any other evening. Alma and Francis played cards together until about 9.30 when Alma kissed her husband goodnight, let Dinah out into the garden and went up to her room. Francis stayed downstairs reading as usual.

About three quarters of an hour later, Irene came home. She went upstairs to her room, but shortly afterwards, feeling hungry, she came back downstairs to find something to eat. As she passed the drawing room she heard deep breathing. Slightly alarmed, she knocked on the door of Francis's room – it was on the ground floor – and went in. It was empty. Irene concluded that he must have fallen asleep in his chair in the drawing room, and reluctant to disturb him, went back to her own bedroom. As she climbed the stairs, she saw George on the landing, leaning over the bannister. He told Irene that he was checking all the lights were out.

Alma came into Irene's room for a while and the two women chatted about their plans for the next day. Alma said she was taking Ratz to Bridport because he was feeling low and needed a break. Then she went back to her own room, leaving Irene to settle down for the night. A night like any other at Villa Madiera.

But not for long. Suddenly Alma burst back into Irene's bedroom. Something terrible had happened. Running downstairs to the drawing room, Irene saw Francis slumped back in his chair, bleeding from a head wound. Alma was distraught, and begged Irene to phone for the doctor. George came in and they carried the unconscious man to his bed. The doctor arrived shortly after eleven and called for a surgeon who in turn called an ambulance. Ratz was taken to a nearby nursing home.

Eventually the police came to the house and tried to question Alma. It was two in the morning by this time and she had been drinking since the attack was discovered. Greatly distressed, she became less and less coherent, and the doctor gave her some morphine so that she could sleep for a while. At six she woke and the detectives began their questioning again.

Alma confessed. Ratz, she said, was depressed and wanted to die. He had been reading a book in which suicide was the theme, and he asked Alma to end it for him. She had struck him with a mallet.

The mallet was found. Alma was charged with attempted murder. She made a statement in which she claimed her husband had dared her to do it.

'He said, "You have not got the guts to do it." I then hit him with the mallet. I hid the mallet outside the house. I would have shot him if I had had a gun.'

Alma was taken first to Bournemouth Police Station and then to Holloway to await trial. It seemed to be a straightforward case, but then two things happened to transform it into headline news.

Firstly, George Stoner took Irene out for a drive in the car to get away from everything for a while. They drove to Wimborne, and on the way back they passed George's parents' house. Quite suddenly, George announced that he had called in there on Sunday evening at about eight o'clock to fetch the mallet – the mallet that was used to strike Francis. He'd worn gloves so that there would be no finger prints. Back at Manor Road that evening, George got very drunk and told Irene, 'Mrs Rattenbury is in jail, and I put her there.'

Secondly, Francis Rattenbury died, and Alma found herself facing a charge not of attempted murder, but of murder.

Irene went to the police to tell them about George's admission. He was arrested and accused together with Alma.

And so began the trial that was the sensation of its time. Everyone had an opinion about it. Alma's defence claimed that her confession

RIGHT **The Posy Tree near Beaminster. It was past this tree that local victims of the Great Plague were carried to a common grave.**

ABOVE **The menacing atmosphere of Dorset on a winter's morning.**

and statement should be disregarded, the one having been made after several hours of steady drinking, the other while she was still befuddled by morphine. George himself gave no evidence. Outside the Old Bailey feelings ran high as the crowd waited for the verdict, and when it came there was almost a riot. Alma was completely absolved, but George was found guilty of murder. Following the solemn custom, the judge put on the black cap and sentenced him to death. He was asked if he had anything to say as to why such a sentence should not be passed. 'Nothing at all, Sir,' was his only reply. Still little more than a boy, George Stoner was taken down to the cells.

The sentence was later commuted to life imprisonment and in all George served only seven years. He was freed in 1942 at the age of 26, having been an exemplary prisoner. He joined the forces, married, and since the war has lived a quiet family life.

Many years have passed since the Rattenbury murder but there is still speculation about what really happened that night at the Villa Madiera. Books, articles – Rattigan's play – have been written about it. Did Alma get away with murder, literally? Did she kill Francis Rattenbury in order to be free to live with George, or was it an act of compassion to end the life which had become a burden to Ratz. Did she persuade George to kill him, or was the lad driven to murder because he was infatuated with Alma and wanted her for himself?

The fact is we will probably never know. George Stoner has steadfastly refused to implicate Alma in any way.

As for Alma herself, the whole series of events proved too much. Although she walked free from the Old Bailey, her life was in ruins and just one week later she killed herself. She went alone to the banks of the River Avon at Christchurch and stabbed herself five times before throwing herself into the water.

She left this poignant note: 'After much walking I have got here ... I tossed a coin, like Stoner always did, and it came down 'Christchurch' ... Pray God nothing stops me tonight ... God bless my children and look after them ... One must be bold to do a thing like this. It is beautiful here, and I am alone. Thank God for peace at last.'

Prehistoric Sites

Dorset's villages are delightful places, neat thatched cottages, tidy brick houses, mellow stone manors, clustered around ponds and greens, bordering leafy lanes, nestling against churches. Everywhere there is a feeling of order and a sense of timelessness. Yet long before the villages existed, before the Normans and the Danes and the Saxons, before even the Romans laid claim to Dorset, its history had already begun. We know Paleolithic man was here — flint tools have been found beside the Frome, the Stour and the Axe as evidence. During the Neolithic period, the chalk downs of Dorset were cultivated and those early farmers left the first lasting structures, burial mounds. You can see them still, the finest being at Pimperne near Blandford. In fact, Dorset is rich in prehistoric sites dating back to Neolithic times and to the Bronze and Iron Ages – burial mounds or barrows, fortifications or rings.

Take for instance the Devil's Nine Rings near Winterbourne Abbas, or the Sacred Circle at Knowlton. There were originally four earthworks at Knowlton; only one, perfectly circular with entrances on opposite sides, remains. Its religious significance in pagan times was immense; later the Christians found this an irresistible challenge and built their own church within the rings to overcome its power once and for all. The church is ruined now – in 1348 the Black Death wiped out the village and without a congregation to serve the church fell into disrepair. Maiden Castle is an even more magnificent collection of rings, an Iron Age fort that expanded into massive ditches and ramparts, particularly spectacular if you can contrive to see it from the air, but just as inspiring to visit on foot.

The barrows and rings have been part of the Dorset landscape for so long that for centuries they must have been taken entirely for granted. Yet down the years, the people who lived and worked and walked beside them must have pondered on the reasons for their

The Sacred Circle at Knowlton.

existence, and puzzled over such mystery. They must also have passed on the stories that have become legends. Who can be surprised that fact becomes a little hazy? For surely such strange places must contain secrets ...

Treasure perhaps – more than one barrow is popularly believed to contain a golden coffin. The oval barrow at Thickthorn Down in the foothills of Cranborne Chase is one. Stuart Piggott of the Royal Commission on Ancient Monuments comprehensively excavated it in 1933. Sadly he found no treasure, nor in fact did he find any burial remains other than a couple of chalk–cut figures. Perhaps the barrow was made for a warrior slain elsewhere. The three round barrows at Cowleaze are also supposed to contain a golden coffin; whether they do or not, we may never know, for it seems that any attempt to investigate further provokes outbursts of thunder and lightning in protest.

One of the earliest barrow diggers, Dr William Sydenham, who lived near Maiden Newton, wrote in 1675 to his uncle in London, telling him of a strange occurrence concerning a barrow at Eggardon Hill near the road to Bridport. As he and his workmen excavated it, casting aside earth full of flints, they came to a part 'perfectly like an oven curiously clayed around' in the middle of which was a perfectly preserved urn full of bones, and a good many black ashes. The most astonishing discovery, however, was that the inside of the oven was hot, causing the first workman to pull back sharply. Dr Sydenham also put in his hand and 'it was warm enough to have baked bread'. More urns were found, and more bones, but no explanation for the heat which Dr Sydenham assumed had endured for centuries.

Equally mysterious, but less sinister, is the belief that music emanates from a Bronze Age burial mound at Culliford Tree between Sutton Poyntz and Broadmayne. Here a number of barrows surround one which in turn supports a clump of beeches, the whole being known as Culliford Tree. The theory is that by lying with your ear to the ground on one of the barrows at precisely midday you will hear a sweet melody. Unfortunately, no-one is sure which barrow is the musical one and sadly, in recent times determined listeners have failed to hear any tune. Perhaps eager barrow diggers have driven away the source of the music; perhaps the hopeful listeners simply haven't employed the correct technique.

Drive north from Wimborne Minster on the road to Blandford Forum and you'll pass through a remarkable avenue of trees – 365 beeches each side of the road, planted it's believed by a woodman on the Kingston Lacy estate. They are a magnificent sight whatever the season. This same road takes you to Badbury Rings close by the beech avenue. Dating back thousands of years, the ramparts and ditches belong to an Iron Age fort built between the sixth century BC and the first century AD. In 43 AD the Roman Second Legion under Commander Vespasian arrived and with their military superiority captured the fort and drove the people out. Strategically, Badbury was an important site, standing at the junction of four roads – to London, Old Sarum, Exeter and Dorchester. Roman civilians lived close by at Vindocladia until the Saxon advance in the middle of the fifth

RIGHT **Arthur, most mysterious of British kings, draws the sword from the stone.**

century. In 901 King Edward the Elder camped here with his army on his way to evict Ethelwold from the manor of Wimborne. Ethelwold, however, fled in the night.

It was 700 years later, in the summer of 1645, that 4000 local shopkeepers, farmers and clergy, known as the Dorset Clubmen, met here to try to get lasting peace between King and Parliament. Later, they met at Hambledon Hill but were broken up by Parliamentary forces.

Badbury was owned by the crown as part of the manor of Kingston Lacy from Saxon times until 1682 when Sir John Banks bought it from the Earl of Newport. In 1982 it was given to the National Trust.

You'll gather from all this that we have a fairly accurate account of the history of Badbury Rings. But one question remains, and it's a question connected with that most mysterious of British Kings, Arthur, whose story is a tapestry of fact and myth, woven together seamlessly so that students of his life are always close to the one, and never far from the other.

We know the Saxon advance was halted towards the end of the fifth century for more than forty years. Some mighty battle stopped them in their tracks. We know too that Arthur defeated the Saxons in the great battle of Mount Badon. Several places claim to be the 'Mons Badanicus' of Arthurian legend. Badbury Rings is one of them. Was it here in the heart of Dorset that the Saxon invaders crumbled before the victorious King? Standing high up on the innermost part, gazing out across the flat countryside which stretches for miles in each direction, it's not hard to persuade yourself that, yes, Arthur did indeed stand here too, 1500 years ago.

In a field above Cerne Abbas lies the figure of a man, 180 feet tall, brandishing a club in his right hand, his left arm outstretched. He's bald, stark naked and extremely well endowed. How he came to be there is a mystery, but for obvious reasons he is regarded as a fertility god. Historians have debated the origins of the Cerne Abbas giant for centuries, although in less liberated times they tended not to mention his most outstanding feature. There are various lines of thought

RIGHT **The King's Guinevere.**

74

about him. One story tells of a giant who roamed the Vale of Blackmore, stealing sheep and eating them. In revenge the local farmers waited one night until he fell asleep – having gorged himself on mutton – pinned him down and killed him. They then cut his outline into the grassy hillside so that everyone would remember how huge he was.

Other stories claim that he was a representation of Hercules, created by the Romans, yet others that he is the native god Cernunnos, which would account for the local place names. Elsewhere he is known by the Celtic name Helith.

Some accounts associate the giant with murder and sacrifice. Thomas Hardy heard that he ate babies – although it has to be said that other unpopular characters were tarred with the same brush,

BELOW **The Cerne Abbas Giant: the figure of a man 180 feet tall.**

Napoleon for instance. It's possible that in Celtic times, human sacrifices were made on the site, the unfortunate victims being herded into the oblong earthwork, known as the Trendle, which you can still see just above the giant's head, before being burnt alive on the figure itself. Even the Romans, not renowned for their squeamishness, were appalled by the sight of huge wickerwork figures packed with men and set alight. Julius Caesar writes of such cruel ceremonies, and how terrible and awesome it must have been to see Helith burning men for the sun god. Hard to believe that the Druids would have overseen such barbaric practices but, as Professor Stuart Piggott points out in his book *The Druids,* ' (they) were the wise men of barbarian Celtic society, and the Celtic religion was their religion, with all its crudities.'

Not surprisingly the most enduring notion attributed to this fine figure of a man is that of fertility god. Some say it's enough for a barren woman simply to visit the giant to be cured; some that a woman should spend a night when the moon is new on his huge phallus asking for his help; others believe that it's necessary for the childless couple to make love there in order to conceive. Certainly there are children running round Dorset today whose parents regard them as proof that the old superstitions work. And such was the giant's reputation for success in these matters, that village maidens not anxious to find themselves pregnant were advised to do their courting elsewhere. The general aura of fecundity was added to each spring when a maypole – itself a symbol of fertility and creation – was erected in the Trendle above the giant.

Incidentally, you may be wondering how local parents, embarrassed by the giant, answered their inquisitive children. Bonny Sartin, of Dorset's famous folk group 'The Yetties' remembers seeing the giant for the first time as he drove past it on a village outing to Weymouth. His mother told him the chalk man on the hillside was a tailor with a pair of scissors in his lap.

One last thought about the giant. There was once a great abbey at Cerne Abbas – the Christian Church liked to make a point at sites of pagan worship – yet it would seem no attempt was ever made to obliterate this bold character. Perhaps the bishops were content to live and let live; perhaps the villagers refused to allow it, too superstitious to risk offending the old gods. Whatever the reason, the fact remains that the monks are now gone, but the Cerne Abbas giant still stands defiant on the hillside.

Bindon Abbey

There's a curious little legend connected with Bindon Abbey, a Cistercian monastery on the banks of the River Frome, not far from Wool. It's the story of a young boy who lived in medieval times, sometimes earning a little money as a swineherd or a bird-scarer. The boy was called Luberlu, and a priest at the abbey, Father de Brian, took him under his wing and, despite the fact that the boy was rather simple, managed to educate him.

One day as Luberlu was walking beside the Frome he met a lovely young girl. She had the most beautiful eyes that seemed to see right into the very heart of him. She appeared beside him as if by magic, stepping out of the rushes that grew along the river bank, and when it was time for Luberlu to return to the abbey, she disappeared just as swiftly. Luberlu was enchanted by her.

They met often, and as spring turned into summer, they fell in love. Luberlu spent more and more time with the mysterious girl; she taught him about the birds and animals who lived by the river, and the plants that grew beside it.

Before too long, Father de Brian began to notice that young Luberlu was neglecting his studies. At first, the kindly priest said nothing but eventually he decided that he must find out what was occupying the boy's mind. Luberlu, too honest and simple for guile, told his old friend everything, how he had met this strange girl, how they spent their time together, and how he loved her with all his heart. As he spoke, the priest realised who she was and sadly he told Luberlu. The girl was a water nymph, he said, haunting the river bank, a being with no soul of her own intent on drawing life from

LEFT **'The girl was a water nymph, he said, haunting the river bank.'**

Luberlu. There could be no happiness, Father de Brian said gently, for Luberlu with his new love.

Luberlu was horrified by what the priest told him. Jumping up, he ran to the river bank to look for the beautiful young girl. But she was nowhere to be found. It was as if she somehow knew that Father de Brian had seen through her trickery. Every day Luberlu walked beside the river, from Wool Bridge to Moreton Ford, calling for his lost love but she had gone. As autumn turned to winter, Luberlu grew more and more unhappy, until his lonely heart broke and he died.

Intrigued by this legend, I wanted to see Bindon Abbey for myself, but very little remains of it today. When we asked a lady who lives nearby for directions, she laughed and told us we were a little late – 400 years too late, in fact. Henry VIII beat you to it, she said. Bindon Abbey was lost in the Dissolution of the Monasteries.

So we went instead to Wool Bridge. It's a stone's throw from the station at Wool, where many a soldier has stepped off the train before making the final leg of the journey to Bovington Recruitment Camp a couple of miles away. Tom Lawrence – Lawrence of Arabia – was stationed at Bovington for some time, and there's now a fine tank museum at the camp.

Beside the bridge itself is a beautiful Jacobean manor house called Woolbridge House. This mellow building with its distinctive chimneys is the seat of the Turbevilles, a very long-established Dorset family. Apparently, the bridge is haunted by a ghostly coach-and-four which drives across it in the evening but it can only be seen by a true Turbeville. Thomas Hardy used this story in his book *Tess of the D'Urbervilles.* Standing on the bridge in the late afternoon sun, gazing down river towards Bindon Abbey, it is easy to picture poor Luberlu and his sweetheart, and to imagine how the abbey looked when it was flourishing.

It seems the abbey had twelve bells to summon the monks to prayer, and according to legend these were moved to three nearby churches after the Dissolution. Four came to Wool, three to Coombe and six to Fordington, the largest one having been re-cast as two.

RIGHT **Thomas Hardy, legendary author and son of Dorset.**

Now whether this came about by design or by skulduggery is not clear, but you can judge for yourself from these lines of doggerel:

Wool Streams and Coombe Keynes Wells
Fordington rogues stole Bindon bells.

Bells were obviously highly prized by Dorset parishioners, for the bell from Knowlton Church, mentioned elsewhere in this book, was also stolen, possibly by the bell-ringers from Sturminster Newton. Whoever the thieves were, they failed in their bid to move the bells to another church. They tried all sorts of tricks to avoid being caught – it was snowing at the time and with great cunning they reversed the horses' shoes to lay a false trail – but they were still very nervous. As they approached the bridge by White Mill, they sent a couple of men on ahead as lookouts. These fellows failed to return, the thieves panicked and tossed the bell over the side of the bridge into the River Stour. And there, by all accounts, the bell remains, some supernatural power thwarting all attempts to retrieve it. More doggerel:

Knowlton bell is stole
And thrown into While Mill Hole
Where all the devils in Hell
Could never pull up Knowlton Bell.

White Mill Bridge is one of the loveliest in Dorset, dating from medieval times. It has little V-shaped spaces along each side to allow pedestrians to move out of the way of the traffic, horses and carts originally of course, motor vehicles now. Like other bridges in the county, including Wool Bridge, it has an important notice on it, stating:

Any person wilfully injuring any part of this county bridge will be guilty of felony and upon conviction liable to be transported for life.

By the Court, T. Fooks.

Mr Fooks was the clerk of the peace. It's also marked '7 & 8 Geo 4 C30 S13' referring to the authorising act of George IV which further

LEFT **'The thieves panicked and tossed the bell over the bridge.'**

ABOVE **The Author standing on the legendary bridge at Sturminster Newton.**

describes the punishment as being 'transported beyond the seas for life or any term not less than seven years' as well as, if the offender is male, 'once twice or thrice publicly or privately whipped ... in addition.'

The signs are faded and Mr Fooks has long since gone. We no longer transport convicts to the colonies. But it has to be said that the bridges are unusually well-preserved and unmarked.

RIGHT **Polly Lloyd on the legendary trail.**

The Cross and Hand

Minterne Magna lies midway between Dorchester and Sherborne, just north of Cerne Abbas and its famous giant. A small upland road runs across Batcombe Down from Minterne to Evershot and about a mile and a half along, close by the crossroads known as Cross and Hand, or Cross in Hand, is a small, rather insignificant pillar. Less than four feet high, the grey stone covered with golden lichen, it would be easy to pass by without taking any notice of it. And yet, for some inexplicable reason, this pillar has more legends attached to it than anywhere else in the county.

Some of the stories connected with this pillar offer quite straightforward explanations as to why it should be there. It's perfectly reasonable to suppose, for example, that it is simply a boundary stone between Sydling and Batcombe, perhaps originally a pillar from a Roman temple. Other folk believe it was a wishing stone, which makes you wonder how many sad or anxious people have come to this lonely place, touched the stone and whispered their hopes and ambitions into the quiet air. Another theory is that the pillar marks an ancient burial place. Minterne had no church, and this spot is within sight of Yetminster, so it would have been a likely choice.

Other stories about the pillar are much more the stuff of legends, capturing the imagination or sending a chill down the spine. There are those who believe that at this very place, four kings crossed hands and swore never to fight again. Did they meet secretly, alone save for a faithful servant each, or was the pledge witnessed by their bravest knights with much pomp and ceremony, shining armour and cloth of gold. What marvellous pictures it conjures up.

RIGHT **'The priest suddenly saw a pillar of fire coming down from heaven . . .'**

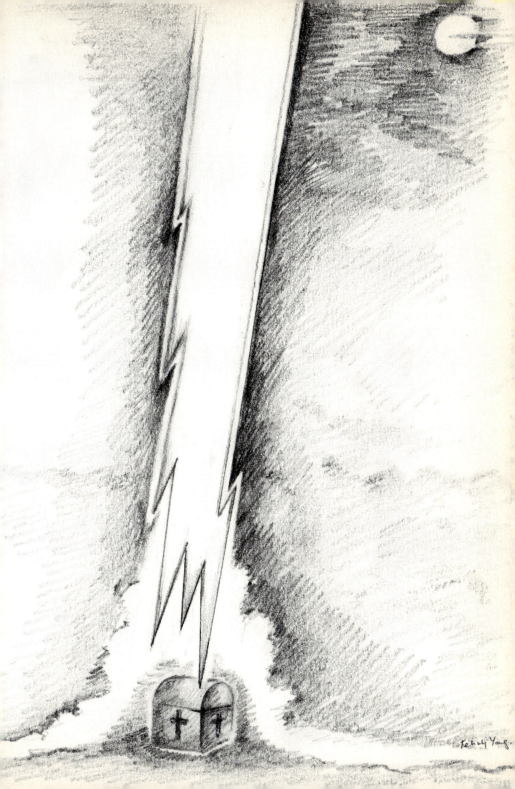

More sinisterly some say a highwayman hid nearby one dark night and sprang out to attack his victim, taking money and life. But he was caught and brought back to the place and hung in chains as a murderer. The pillar is a reminder of both the crime and the punishment.

There's another story about a man from Cerne who went over to Batcombe and stole a sheep. In order to carry the creature home, he tied its legs together and slung it round his neck. The sheep was heavy and the thief soon grew tired, so he sat down on the pillar to rest. Perhaps it was just retribution, perhaps it was a cruel blow of fate, but as he sat there, the animal struggled to free itself and slipped from his shoulders. The rope tightened around his neck and the unfortunate man was strangled. The sheep survived, the rustler died.

Thomas Hardy mentions this lone pillar twice in his writing. A passage in *Tess of the D'Urbervilles* says that it was put up by the family of some miscreant who was tortured and hung for his misdeeds, and who, having sold his soul to the Devil, haunts the place. In his poem *The Lost Pyx* Hardy relates another legend which tells why the stone pillar exists. It's the story of a priest in the Middle Ages who set off to administer the Last Rights to a dying man. Along the way, he lost the pyx which contained the Holy Sacrament. Retracing his steps along the lonely road, the priest suddenly saw a pillar of fire coming down from heaven to where the pyx lay on the ground. Cattle and wild animals knelt all around and the priest raised the stone we see today to commemorate the miracle.

We may never know the real significance of the lone pillar at Cross in Hand. Perhaps all these stories are true, perhaps none of them are. Perhaps its biggest claim to fame is the fact that there are so many legends attached to it. And for some, that is the greatest mystery of all.

Saints

Since the days of the old gods, and probably even before then, water has been believed to have mystical properties. More than simply a sustainer of life to man, beast and plant, there has always been the suspicion that water has the power to heal and bring good luck. It seems to be inbred in us still; even in these sophisticated times, people almost instinctively throw coins into ponds and fountains.

Natural springs were frequently used as pagan shrines; Christianity simply took them over, or moved in so that the shrines became Christian by association. Even baptism is a ritual adopted from an older religion.

In Dorset there are many springs and wells that have taken the name of some saint or other. Stachy's Well, for instance, in the delightful village of Ibberton, is named after Saint Eustachius, the name shortened for convenience. He was a Roman general, martyred for turning to Christianity. The water in the well comes from a spring just below the church which stands high up looking out over Blackmore Vale and which is also dedicated to the saint. Some time ago the Water Board changed the well to a reservoir and piped the water down to the village, the pure spring water coming out of a tap opposite the pub.

When King Edward was murdered at Corfe Castle by his step-mother Elfrida in 978 AD, she hid his body in a well where it lay undiscovered for a year. Miraculously the water remained pure, and the King's corpse remained intact; small wonder that 'St Edward's Fountain' became a place of pilgrimage for those seeking a cure for their physical and spiritual ills.

And at Cerne Abbas, in the churchyard, is the well of St Augustine. Cerne Abbas is a classic example of a pagan site being taken over by Christians, with the huge chalk figure of the Cerne Abbas Giant looking down on the abbey. Augustine was the first

ABOVE **Cerne Abbas well of St Augustine.**

LEFT **St Blanche was a Breton saint who was
kidnapped by pirates and escaped by walking
home across the water.**

Archbishop of Canterbury, sent to Britain with 40 monks by Pope
Gregory in 596 AD. He journeyed throughout the country spreading
the Christian religion, and visited Cerne Abbas. Apparently, he
destroyed the 'great local idol' – presumably the giant – which
infuriated those who worshipped it. Converting heathens is evidently
hard work and the band of evangelists felt weary and thirsty, so
St Augustine dug his wooden staff into the ground and up sprang a
crystal clear fountain. As they refreshed themselves, the irate locals
surrounded them and attacked them in a rather unusual fashion.
They pinned cows' tails onto their clothes, and with much jeering and
ridicule, drove them out of Cerne Abbas.

As a punishment, St Augustine laid a curse on the villagers, and
those who had abused him sprouted tails themselves. For many years
afterwards it was believed that anyone who spoke against Augustine
would find himself in a similar predicament.

Meanwhile, the well became a sacred place and until the

seventeenth century was a proper shrine dedicated to St Augustine and visited by many pilgrims. New-born babies were taken there at sunrise to be dipped in the waters.

Another name for that well is the Silver Well, so named because St Edwold, who was led to it by a premonition after the Danes killed his brother the King, gave some silver coins to a shepherd who happened to be there at the time. It is said that at Easter, the faces of those about to die can be seen in the well.

The earliest book ever written about Dorset was called *A Survey of Dorsetshire*. Published in 1732 and attributed by some to John Coker, it is believed to have been written earlier, in the 1620s by a man called Thomas Gerard. In it is mentioned the town of

Whitechurch which took name from one St White, a virgin martyr whose well the Inhabitants will show you not farre off in the side of an hill.

This well is in the parish of Stanton St Gabriel and is known as St Vita's Well, or St Candida's Well. Once again the water is believed to have healing properties – particularly good for sore eyes if visited at daybreak. The local name for periwinkles growing on the hillside is St Candida's Eyes. Tradition calls for bent pins to be thrown into the well, accompanied by this chant:

Holy well, holy well,
Take my gift and cast a spell.

The saint herself has a number of names. Her true name was St Wite which is sometimes given as Wita or Vita. But another corruption, St White, has led to her being associated with the colour, hence she is also called St Blanche, St Gwen or St Candida, all names meaning white.

St Blanche was a Breton saint who was kidnapped by English pirates and escaped by walking back home across the water, a feat she performed again later to help vanquish another band of Englishmen. In West Dorset the white line that seems to divide the tides on a flat sea is known as St Wite's Tail – the French call it St Blanche's Causeway.

RIGHT **The shrine of St Wite.**

But it is more likely that St Wite was a Saxon holy lady murdered by the Danes in the ninth century. Around this time, hermits both male and female were not uncommon and indeed played an important role. They acted as coastguards, lighting beacons, they helped travellers and were respected by the local community.

The Church of St Candida and Holy Cross at Whitchurch Canonicorum near Bridport is a country church with a square tower. It is quite remarkable because it is one of only two churches in the entire country which contain a shrine that has survived the Reformation intact. The other is admittedly much more famous – it is the shrine of Edward the Confessor in Westminster Abbey.

St Wite's shrine dates from the thirteenth century, and is built of the local golden stone. The upper part, the tomb, contains the saint's relics; the lower part which supports it, has three oval openings in it. The bones lie within a lead casket inscribed in Latin – *Hic REQESCT RELIQE SCE WITE* – here lie the relics of St Wite. In 1900 the tomb split open and it was possible to examine the reliquary and its

contents, the bones of a small woman aged about 40. It seems it had been opened before, probably in the sixteenth century.

It is a wonder, indeed perhaps it is a miracle, that the shrine escaped desecration. It appears to have been visted for cures rather than purely devotional purposes. Pilgrims would have lit candles and touched the shrine, thrusting their hands or feet or head into the oval openings in the stone. Handkerchieves would have been smoothed against the stone and carried back to those too sick to make the journey. Prayers and messages would have been written down and left inside it.

The Reformation ended pilgrimages. Edward VI banned 'shrines, candlesticks, trindles, rolls of wax, pictures and all other monuments of feigned miracles ... vain and abominable and most damnable before God'. But somehow the shrine of St Wite survived. Perhaps it was moved to a safe place and then quietly returned at a later date. However it was achieved, this quiet country church succceded in preserving it.

Today visitors still come to see St Wite's tomb, some out of curiosity, others with more of a sense of pilgrimage. Candles flicker and the mellow stone cavities are lined with scraps of paper asking for her blessing. The image of St Wite, martyred by the Viking invaders who sailed in strange shaped boats, is captured in the tapestry cover of a long narrow hassock in front of the shrine.

All old churches are filled with an air of timelessness; at Whitchurch Canonicorum more than most it is possible to reach out across the countless years and touch history.

RIGHT 'At Whitchurch Canonicorum more than most it is possible to reach out across the countless years and touch history.'

Also Available

GHOSTS OF DORSET
by Peter Underwood
Explores a whole range of hauntings. A ghostly white donkey, a world-famous screaming skull, a phantom coach-and-horses story which Thomas Hardy used in *Tess of the D'Urbervilles* and a prehistoric 'Peeping Tom' are only some of the subjects. We meet a phantom army, visit a town with a dozen haunted houses – and learn of Lawrence of Arabia making ghostly appearances in Dorset.

MYSTERIOUS PLACES
by Peter Underwood
Visits locations that 'seem to have been touched by a magic hand'. The man who has been called Britain's No. 1 ghost hunter reflects: 'We live in a very mysterious world ...'
'... an insight into some of the more mysterious places in the south west.'
David Elvidge, Launceston & Bude Gazette

SUPERNATURAL ADVENTURE
by Michael Williams
Contains a great deal of unpublished material relating to the Supernatural.
'Spiritual healing, automatic writing are just a few of the spectrum of subjects ... neat, well-presented ... easy-to-read volume.'
Psychic News

WESTCOUNTRY MYSTERIES
Introduced by Colin Wilson
A team of authors probe mysterious happenings in Somerset, Devon and Cornwall. Drawings and photographs all add to the mysterious content.
'A team of authors have joined forces to re-examine and probe various yarns from the puzzling to the tragic.'
James Belsey, Bristol Evening Post

HIDDEN KNOWLEDGE
by Lori Reid
Lori Reid in her debut for Bossiney traces the origins of many great festivals and occasions in the calendar.
'... charmingly written and presented ... Lori Reid delves the mysteries and origins of our heritage, some spiritual, some legend – to enlighten and fascinate the reader on the journey through the year.'
Della Powell, The North Cornwall Advertiser

We shall be pleased to send you our catalogue giving full details of our growing list of titles for Devon, Cornwall, Dorset and Somerset and forthcoming publications. If you have difficulty in obtaining our titles, write direct to Bossiney Books, Land's End, St Teath, Bodmin, Cornwall.